12-26-74

-26-74

# I Really Want to Feel Good About Myself!

# I REALLY WANT TO FEEL GOOD ABOUT MYSELF!

Poems by Former Drug Addicts

selected by

**Lee Bennett Hopkins**

**and Sunna Rasch**

THOMAS NELSON INC., PUBLISHERS
Nashville, Tennessee / New York, New York

*First edition*

Library of Congress Cataloging in Publication Data

Hopkins, Lee Bennett, comp.
    I really want to feel good about myself!

    1. American poetry—20th century. I. Rasch, Sunna, joint comp. II. Title.
PS615.H6        811'.5'408        74–10283
ISBN 0–8407–6411–1

To all of us
who are Halfway
between what we are
and what we can become

# Contents

9

# I Really Want to Feel Good About Myself!

# Introduction

They did not think of themselves as poets. They were too busy working out the pain that had put them in the rehabilitation center in the first place. They thought everybody on the "outside" had it made.

I was on the outside, but by the time my "drug kids," as I called them, and I got under way, we were all insiders! Whatever it is that binds people together, we had it. If I had to give it a name, I would call it trust.

They were on a stiff rehabilitation program in Samaritan Village in South Fallsburg, New York, and I thought poetry would help them. The directors were skeptical at first, but decided to give it a try.

Enrollment was voluntary. The course took its own shape. It wasn't my course—it was ours. It grew out of the students' individual motivations and need to express themselves.

After the first session, we needed a larger room. There were fourteen in the group, ranging in age from fifteen to twenty-seven. Some came out of curiosity at first, or because the class was a break in a stringent work routine. After a few weeks the poetry session had become a privilege. I was not aware of it until one student was suspended briefly as a punishment. For infractions in other departments the program directors might take away someone's privilege to go swimming, but they punished one of our group by not letting him share in the poetry class.

But so it was.

Out of the students' pain and their wrestling with themselves came a knowing, a wisdom that surfaced in their writings. One person's light kindled the next. Soon I began to receive more and more of what we called gut poetry. One day I was so impressed that I said, "These poems are good enough to be published."

Peter, one of the group, grinned and picked it right up. "Yeah," he said, "but do you *really* think so?"

That's how this book came to be.

Being too close to the situation, I approached Lee Bennett Hopkins. He and I began to cull through hundreds of poems that had been written by the group between November, 1970, and November, 1971. Some of the students are using pseudonyms, but their feelings are printed here just as they recorded them.

The class began writing in November, 1970. A year later all had departed from the upstate house; eleven were back in downstate Re-Entry in Samaritan Halfway Society in Jamaica, New York, where they were being graduated from the program. The age listed for each one is that at the time the poetry was written.

Today they are all back in society, determined to make a contribution to the world, each in his own way. I still hear from them.

At our last meeting in the fall of 1971, when graduation was imminent, we spoke seriously about their future, and I asked them what they wanted most out of life. In so many words, each told me the same thing:

"I really want to feel good about myself."

Sunna Rasch
Monticello, New York

14

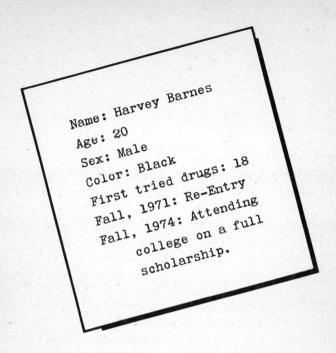

Name: Harvey Barnes
Age: 20
Sex: Male
Color: Black
First tried drugs: 18
Fall, 1971: Re-Entry
Fall, 1974: Attending
college on a full
scholarship.

## Reflections

*In a world of communism, atheism, catechism, and complete cynicism, I've begun to wonder where the hell do I go from here. Peace.*

## Love

It don't do nothing for me
But cause pain, lost dreams, and futile hopes.
Hopes of spring days, starry nights, moonlit skies, tender lips,
    warm thighs.
Yeah, but I might be wrong.
It could be the warmth and tenderness of someone who cares
    for you;
Times you can look back at, smile and remember as happy
    days.
I guess you can't always tell when you're in love.


## Mother!

What's a mother?
It could mean a complete social institution—
Could be!
Is it the thing that develops young America
Or is it the thing that takes away my manhood?
Could be!
I think the people that spout the land of the free and the home
    of the brave are mothers!
Up against the wall, you
Jive mother!

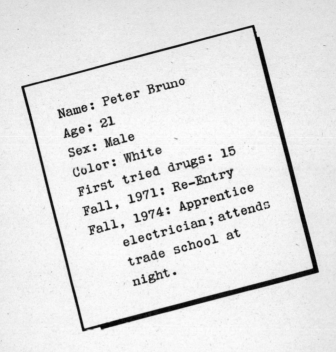

```
Name: Peter Bruno
Age: 21
Sex: Male
Color: White
First tried drugs: 15
Fall, 1971: Re-Entry
Fall, 1974: Apprentice
        electrician; attends
trade school at
night.
```

## Reflections

*I'm twenty-one years old. Most of the time I feel like thirty-five. I'm an ex-drug addict. Most people prefer to use the word* junkie *or* dope fiend—*but whatever you call it, the end result is the same. You see, I don't have to die to see what Hell is like.*

*I come from an average, white, middle-class family; I have three brothers and two sisters. I was the middle child. I started using hard narcotics at sixteen. I was seventeen when I spent my first holiday in Rikers Island Penitentiary.*

17

*Somewhere in between then and now, the court system had my back against the wall and made me go into Samaritan Halfway Society, a drug addiction agency.*

That was to be the factor that helped me make my positive flip back into society. I graduated from Samaritan and became a staff member there.

Now I am an apprentice electrician in Local 7. "From a dope fiend to a hard hat." (WOW! How much more can I reenter society?)

I never thought I would someday become a construction worker. It just didn't seem to fit in with my life-style, my values. But when money became tight, it was either steal or work. I'm not shooting any more dope, so I work. Simple, isn't it? Sometimes it seems so simple that it bores the hell out of me.

I realize that the world didn't change, only I did.

Now I got a label: ex-addict. People know me and refer to me by that.

Pretty shitty way to become a conversation piece, ain't it?

## Philosophy

To look *at* a man and form an opinion of him by what you
　　*see*
Instead of looking *into* a man and forming an opinion of him
　　by what you *feel*
Is one of the greatest sins man has ever committed.

# Who's the Lame?

He wasn't saying much.
He really wasn't nobody that meant nothing.
After all, a guy who would pack tomatoes for a living can't
    have too much going for him.

But I was cool . . .
   Wall Street hipster
   Vigorous and vined
Jazz and Junk
"Come on, little bro, let me take you on Broadway."
   Little Bro Joe, my man.
Just got word he got a woman
   Got a gig
   Got a short
   Got some vines
   Reefer and wine
   Ski motels on weekends
   Partying in between.
I just got a NO on my request to go home for 24 fuckin' hours.
So who's the LAME?

# So Real

If you could wear my eyes
Just for a little while
It would be so much better, so much easier.
Heart beats like heart,
but on different levels.
Yet eyes seek other eyes
and sparkle together.
Nature is real!

Nature is warm!
Nature is natural!
And yet we, who are nature's productions,
Created instinctively and unconditioned,
End up as molded creations of a totally incompetent, unfeel-
    ing, unjust system.

And the glow diminishes slowly and painfully
Until the eye meets the sparkle of another
And the soul is rejuvenated.


## Cut Me Loose

Cut me loose!
Let me run barefoot
through the fields of blossoming flowers.
Let the warm rays of sunshine
seep into my naked pores
and warm my soul.

Cut me loose!
Let me cast out my wings
and soar recklessly to the heavens,
swan-dive into the Tiber River,
swim to the shore and loll in the
sands of the Garden of Eden.

Cut me loose!
To let my freak flag fly
and let my hair hang down.
Let me fill these still, quiet eves
with the sound of my songs of life and love.
And when my throat gets parched from my music making
I shall drink from the ocean of life,

Embracing its tart taste as boldly
as I would embrace its sweetness.

Cut me loose!
Unlock the shackles that restrain my soul from freedom
and let the world be *mine*
For the taking. . . .


## Fear

FEAR is that troubled, worried, anxious feeling you get
    after you've just given your last ten dollars
(against your better judgment)
to the connection.
"Give me the money and wait here."
And you're sick.
    You sweat.
    Waves of nausea ripple your guts
    Eyes water
    Nose runs
    Legs ache
    And you wait
        and wait
            and wait. . . .
Praying to God
that he's coming back.

FEAR is that increasing insecure feeling you have
as you roll into Rikers Island for the first time.
"Block Two: Waters, Armstrong, Bruno, Barnwell."
And the queens go crazy. . . .
Keys jingle, jangle, clickle, clackle.
I wonder if they see the fear on my face.
Oh, my God!

They aren't going to put me in the Day Room
with all these fucking maniacs — are they?
Need a smoke
Holy shit!
One of the M.O.'s tried to yoke me as I passed his cell.
He's crazy! He's insane!
Oh, Ma,
Please get me out of here.
You can't imagine how it is here.
The dude I sleep with smells like death.
I swear he's hummin'
And I think he wants to fuck me. . . .
Get me out of here. . . .
PLEASE. . . .
          PLEASE . . .
                    PLEASE. . . .


## Beyond

I've wanted to walk through Central Park
In autumn, birds singing, just before dark.
Sitting there by the side of the pond,
Feet soaking, mind at ease, thoughts traveling far beyond.
Beyond the filth out there in the street,
to Botanical Garden, where the smell is sweet.
Beyond the prejudices and hypocrisy of others,
to a place where all men are treated like brothers.
Beyond the dope and degeneracy,
to peace, love, and empathy.
Beyond the rat race nine to five,
Where man must learn how to fight to survive.
To a place where man is *happy* to be alive
To a place where man is *happy* to be alive.

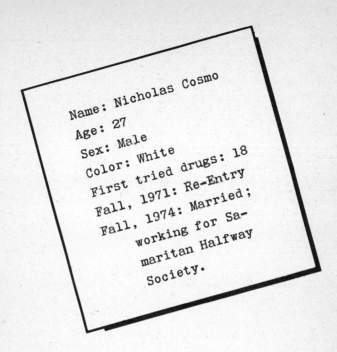

```
Name: Nicholas Cosmo
Age: 27
Sex: Male
Color: White
First tried drugs: 18
Fall, 1971: Re-Entry
Fall, 1974: Married;
    working for Sa-
    maritan Halfway
    Society.
```

## Reflections

*How do I speak about myself after so many years
have gone down the drain—in my case, in the cooker?
I had the run-of-the-mill childhood with a little dash
of Italian conditioning thrown in. I went to parochial
school, then to high school for about two years. When
I was sixteen, my ma and pa broke up. At that time
I felt that I wanted to be the so-called man of the
house. Big deal! I was about eighteen when I was do-
ing it to myself, with pills, pot, snappers, junk; var-
ious different poisons under various different names.
Take your pick. All the years after that consist of*

scheming, hustling, robbing here and there, wherever my hand could get, sometimes falling into something nice, and then, out of it. I get sick when I think about all that pain and self-destruction.

Then, in the summer of 1970, after almost dying from a train accident that I caused myself because of dope, I found my way, with the help of my mother, to a strange place in the sun called Samaritan Village. I've been here to date twenty-one months. I'm in Re-Entry, living out and working for the program. I choose to work for it because it is so little to give back for my life, and I know where it's at, it was my (and I'll spell it out) L-I-F-E. Right now, I am awaiting graduation. I have a girl named Chris whom I love like the stars love the night, have people and just about everything I need for the time being. I've got respect and love, and that's far out. It's all right now.

Don't always look outward, sometimes
    there is very little to find.
Take a look inward, there is a lot to find.
You can see it if you want to,
You can see it if you try.
So don't get hung up on the outside,
Get hung up too long there and your inside will die.

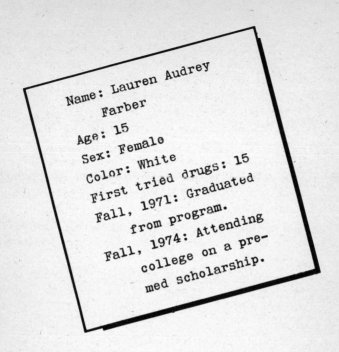

Name: Lauren Audrey
      Farber
Age: 15
Sex: Female
Color: White
First tried drugs: 15
Fall, 1971: Graduated
      from program.
Fall, 1974: Attending
      college on a pre-
      med scholarship.

## Reflections

*Damned for being right and cursed for being wrong*
*With the pain and love you feel yourself being torn*
*Not knowing where to stand and standing nowhere*
*Wanting to run and not running from fear.*

*I want to love someone with someone loving me*
*But not knowing and wondering if ever that will be.*

## What For?

*What for?*
   Don't question.
*Why not?*
   Because—
   You can't think.
*Why not?*
   Because—
   It corrupts.
*Corrupts what?*
   The system.
*What system?*
   Our way of life.
*Is this life?*


## I

Will you cross the rillows with me
Over lopsided shapes of reality—
Past the cemented flowers,
Past the painted sun,
Past the grayed sky,
Escaping the nevers of always,
As two being one?

Will you rest your head against my chest,
Open up your toy box,
Play with your dusted dreams
Of wandering through sand castles
Or searching for pirates' treasure,
Where time has no meaning
And there is no past?

Will you follow me in mystries shadows
Through a fire's flickering light
Or the ocean's endless waves,
Laughing when it rains,
Smiling with the night,
Never letting me go
In your mind's gaze?

## II

Drops of dew on a blade of grass,
The rain on a pane of glass,
Fireflies that brighten the night,
Birds in early morning flight,
Buttercups beneath your chin,
A child's eyes smile within.
Take a step past you,
Rest, your work is through.
It's your turn to dream
Of castles made of ice cream.
Run with a breeze
And laugh with the trees—
You are free
And I am me.

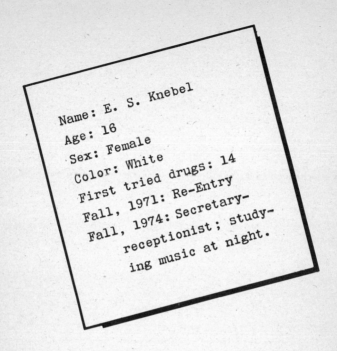

Name: E. S. Knebel
Age: 16
Sex: Female
Color: White
First tried drugs: 14
Fall, 1971: Re-Entry
Fall, 1974: Secretary-
  receptionist; study-
  ing music at night.

## Reflections

*Before long, I will no longer be a teen-ager. There will be no excuse for my uncontrollable energy, I am told, for it will not be acceptable then.*

*But I have an insatiable thirst for learning and for life, offset by a depressing fear of growing old, possibly because I see my elders lose their motivations and interest along with their youth.*

*I've been told to slow down and relax, that I'll see more and in greater detail. I say, leave the detail for those with time to enjoy it. I am the only one*

29

*here who will make my life spicy, so leave the bland*
*things to those who only wanted.*

*I'm growing hard with exposure. I suppose it's inevitable, but at the same time trying to retain my sensitivity is giving me a lot of pain.*

*What drives me the strongest is my number-one conviction, which is where I get my motivation. I believe that the only reason I've been put on this earth is to have as good a time as I possibly can—or at least until my strength gives out.*

*Perhaps it is too selfish an idea to base my life upon—but I would not be happy under any other circumstances and I will not have Me any other way.*

So you led another on,
So you got taken again, didn't you?
Little fool.
So you let another one promise you the sun, the moon, the
    stars.
Yeah, you got them—the promises, I mean.
But that's O.K.
You still smile
And walk with your head tilted up,
You know the way—
"Defiance" herself!
But you don't fool me,
I know the pain.
We're alike—you and I
Both of us fall for the same thing—
But I'm different from the rest—oh—very different
'Cause I'm the one who loves you.

# Queen Machine

Down the long expanse of hall
 She came walking.
Calmly, expressionless,
 Like a cool blue goddess
Out of an ancient myth.

She looked at me,
 Then beyond me,
Staring back into her considerable past.
 Her eyes then registered warmness for my benefit
And, as required, her mouth so cool and blue
Said
 Hell-o

```
Name: Thomas McKinney
Age: 22
Sex: Male
Color: Black
First tried drugs: 16
Fall, 1971: Working with
          prisoners on Riker's
          Island while in
          Re-Entry
Fall, 1974: Assistant
          director of INTAKE,
          a division of Wild-
          cat Service Corpora-
          tion, an employment
          program for ex-addicts.
```

## Reflections

*In this complex and abstract society there are a great
many things we overlook—things that often point out
the underlying hypocrisy of which we are constantly
a part. One of these tools of deceit is the correctional
and rehabilitation system to which we condemn our
fellowman, who is a product of this bizarre society.*

*It has been rigidly instilled in us, since early child-
hood, that to make a mistake is something bad, and
as a result we try to hide or rationalize away our
mistakes instead of facing them and trying to change*

33

them. The same thing holds true with the correctional system. The so-called misfits are society's mistakes and the prisons are where the mistakes are hidden, under the guise of rehabilitation. These human beings are locked away, tortured, denied basic human rights, and are expected to change. Most of them do change . . . for the worse! Either I have a misconception of the word "rehabilitation," or the leaders of my treasured society are all bureaucratic liars.

Cruelty doesn't induce change. The problem and its source, not the result, must be dealt with. A man can't be forced to change; he must first want to change and accept the necessity for change.

I've heard it said by a number of people that they are concerned with property rights, social liberties, and economic progress. But what about the lives of the people vegetating in our penal institutions?

Those of us who accept this assault on humanity should take a serious look at our values, for when we forget about mankind we are forgetting about ourselves!


## To Love

To love is to live,
For man without love
Is like a soul
Without a spirit.
Just like the warm spring breeze
brings life to the seemingly lifeless vine,
So love brings forth a fresh awakening and relevance
From the depths of man.
It inspires man to the essence

34

and fulfillment of his desires
and to the attainment
of his dreams.

Snow could not exist without cold,
nor could heat exist
without fire.
Man is like the snow and the heat—
Love is the horn of plenty
from which he picks his life-sustaining fruits,
the fruits of happiness, joy, and peace.
His love is his happiness,
His happiness is his joy,
And his joy is his peace.

The ultimate achievement for man
Is to be happy in love.
I, being part of man, am involved
in a soul-searching quest.
A quest that may lead me down many a hard and winding
    road
with obstacles that at times seem unbearable.
But in the midst of my confusion,
when I reflect on that for which I strive,
I am renewed with a strong sense of direction.
Love is my motivation and my reward!

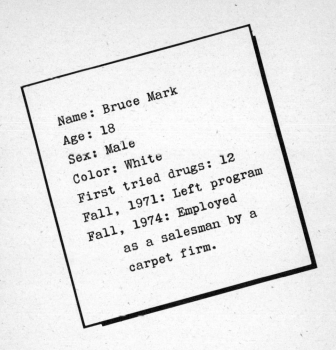

Name: Bruce Mark
Age: 18
Sex: Male
Color: White
First tried drugs: 12
Fall, 1971: Left program
Fall, 1974: Employed
   as a salesman by a
   carpet firm.

## Reflections

*This is in memory of all those perfect, upright citizens who are superhuman and love their fellow man.*

*While in Samaritan, the stress and strain of emotional feelings were always present, but the cutthroat attitude of people was almost never apparent.*

*You know, it's funny . . . the dark, shadowy dope fiend who learns in alleys has more compassion and warmth than the average person walking in the street. All those people out there who point the*

37

*fingers should be put into a model world to see who would survive, they or the mutants.*

Don't get me wrong. I'm not blaming my mistake on anyone but myself. In fact, I use all those hypocrites as an incentive. I'm sorry, but it would take a book that could never be finished to explain my feelings. Man is such a complicated creature. Thank God, there are a few decent ones left. Not perfect, mind you, but decent.

P.S. All you hypocrites. Be sure to remember me in your prayers.

## What Is the Definition of an Animal?

From what I've learned
From being taught
By qualified people,
(Now that's a thought!)
I made a mistake
And had to pay
By living with torture
From day to day.
They put me on an island
In the River East
In a cage with another beast.

We were sent out to play
For a couple of hours a day.
We stayed in little groups
And fought.
Riots and hunger strikes
Were our entertainment,
We had curses for compliments
And cruelty for love.

They looked on in wonderment
As if not to know
Why we beasts
Would push and shove.

I loved this so much
That I came back thrice.
"It's funny how nothing changes,"
I thought, while I ate my rice—
It's called rehabilitation
And costs people a pretty price
And they pay their money in hope of change.
I can't understand this,
To me it's strange.
To fight fire with fire
Is such an inhuman desire.
Will anyone listen to someone
Who was once a beast
Or will rehabilitation
Carry on with the feast?


## If I May and if I Might

People tell of a Supreme Being.
They go to church and breathe His name,
They talk of angels,
But it's all the same—
They pray for pity,
Bow in shame,
Talk of brothers and sisters,
Speak of beauty and wonder,
And throw knives at one another.
But if I may and if I might,
Please spare me, Lord, from this fight.

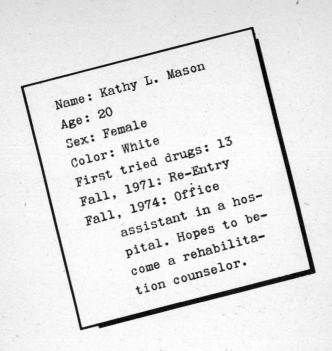

Name: Kathy L. Mason
Age: 20
Sex: Female
Color: White
First tried drugs: 13
Fall, 1971: Re-Entry
Fall, 1974: Office
   assistant in a hos-
   pital. Hopes to be-
   come a rehabilita-
   tion counselor.

## Reflections

*They didn't think I'd live. Waiting, hoping, and wish-
ing I'd pull through, only four pounds—poor thing,
but thanks to science I made it, only to come into
this world and thirteen years later wondering if I was
going to live. It was a vicious merry-go-round and I
wondered when I'd pull the ring and win. At thirteen
I was already a conditioned product of parochial
school. At fourteen I was asked to leave for fighting
in the streets with my school uniform on; it was bad
for the business. I had already been drinking, hang-*

ing out in parks, and getting a reputation of being a loudmouth and crazy.

By the time I was fifteen I was smoking grass. There was this guy Frankie who was coming to school with long hair and wearing blankets. He first turned me on to pot and Dylan. Soon I began cutting school, hanging out in the poolroom and getting high. Not too many girls hung out with the guys, but I had an H.O. card. Then one night someone came around with acid and I decided to try a mind-expanding trip. I felt like a hyena after I took it and I dug the fantasy world I had for myself. Some people daydream; I made my dreams reality. I started tripping heavy until one day the acid was too strong and I flipped out. It was really a bummer. I looked like an escapee from Creedmor as they wheeled me into the first of many institutions to come. They admitted me to the psycho ward, and if I wasn't crazy I would be by the time I got out. All of my possessions were taken away. My resentment for authority was really starting to build. They gave us medicine to keep us knocked out so we wouldn't give any trouble. I was good. The nurses liked me and so I talked them into not giving me so much medication so I could get my head together. Sugar is like gold, so I saved my sugar and asked the girls to make a big ruckus when my mother came. I promised to give them my sugar. They did and my mom signed me out the next day.

I had quit school and been on probation. My people were taking me to court for being a juvenile delinquent because they couldn't manage me. When the court saw the hospital report they decided that I needed help. They sent me to a training school for girls. It was run by nuns—back under their thumb! I was a troublemaker and I always managed to get caught. Around that time I was getting an education

42

as far as schoolwork and girls living with girls. This one girl, Sue, who looked better than some guys I knew, was always playing with my hair and telling me how pretty I was. It made me nervous but I also liked it. I received a letter saying that my boyfriend had deserted me for another girl and I decided to cover up the hurt with Sue. At fifteen I took the affections of a girl—a girl who believed she was a boy —in place of my hurt. Survival makes people do funny things.

After ten months I split on my visit home. When I got out I got a job and began shooting speed to lose weight because I was 120 pounds; my hair was cut real short from my previous role in the training school. Nobody recognized me. I lost 30 pounds. The working world wasn't so bad when I was high. I could actually laugh about being squashed like a sardine on the subway. But my demented brain couldn't handle speed too long 'cause I was staying up for weeks at a time. My liver was really bad and I was getting paranoid and scared of myself. All this while I was telling myself I'd never use dope—the big stuff—I would never be a junkie. But one night I was tired of the high I was getting and my nerves were shot. So I decided to shoot some heroin to calm down. I mainlined because I had been already using the needle when I shot speed. Well, I puked my guts out, but after the sickness I felt a strange glowy feeling, I was relaxed and everything looked rosy. All the hassles of the world were a million miles away, and that's just where I wanted them to stay. That's when I met Louie and started on my heroin run. And that was the beginning of the end.

I worked a little until I had so bad a habit that I needed money and I'd do anything just to buy that bag of salvation. I didn't care how or where I got it, only that I had this drug that made everything all right. Mother's Day was the first time I got arrested. I was so stoned that the reality of the scene didn't hit me until I woke up with iron bars staring me in the face. I felt like a caged animal. You're allowed one phone call when you get busted, so I called my people to ask them to bail me out of this hell. I got a stub back from the telephone operator and on the answer was written "No"—that's all—one great big disappointing "No". I had no tissues, so I blew my nose in the stub. I stayed there on a charge of loitering because my boyfriend took the weight. But I rotted two months because I didn't have the fifty-dollar bail.

Someone once said you meet more characters in jail than anywhere else; whoever said it must have been there. There were more misfits, freaks, and lesbians than in a freak show. What did I care? I felt like I fit in—I had a tattoo of A+ on my finger, some abscesses on my arms from missing shots, I was only 90 pounds soaking wet, and I had just finished kicking a habit. My case just kept getting postponed. There were some Quakers in the building trying to rehabilitate the junkies, so I went to their program, figuring that it would be easier to split that way. When I returned home I was worse off than when I went in. I didn't last long at my house; I was cleaning them out and they wondered what would go next. I went to live with my girlfriend, her son, and the roaches. I started looking like a skid. I never ate, my only thoughts were to satisfy this monkey clawing at my back. I didn't even get high anymore. I needed stuff just to make me feel normal and so I wouldn't get sick. I tried methadone, but that only held me until I could get enough money to cop again. One day some guy came and arrested me and sentenced me to the Rockefeller program, which is the same as the

*Women's House of Detention; only this jail was sup-*
*posed to be a rehabilitation center. I conned a priest*
*to get me out of there and into his program. This*
*trip I stayed two weeks.*

*After I left I went back to my old routine of getting*
*high, getting busted. Finally my back was against the*
*wall. I got busted again and I didn't want to go back*
*to jail, so I decided to make a go of it, stick it out in*
*this program or just kill myself if I had the nerve.*

*Now, half a liver later, after completing a program*
*which was really a school of life, I find that living*
*ain't so bad after all and you know what? I can laugh*
*—and I don't have to be high!*

## The Women's House of Detention

There is a dungeon in the city, a pitiful place to be,
But if you've broken a law, they'll leave you at the door
Of The Women's House of D.

The judge had no sympathy,
The bail was much too high;
They took my fingerprints, photographed my face,
And took me to this horrible place
Called the Women's House of D.

They ask if you are well and lock you in a cell.
The beds are made of iron and there's no use crying
'Cause nobody will hear you.

It doesn't matter what color you are,
Or what kind of crime you commit.
The rats and roaches will infest your cell
And keep you company.

45

I just came back from the courtroom,
They postponed the case again
The legal aid was there—it's good to have a friend.

But now the ugly wagon comes, to take me to my cell—
I'm going back to prison to spend some time in hell.


## Danny

I'm afraid to let you know—
I'm afraid you'll hurt me.

My love is too confused . . . too complicated,
I can't be sure.

These feelings are driving me mad.
I want to feel, to relate, to touch, to smell you,
Just to be close and have you around.

A little log cabin,
Fireplace and marshmallows,
The dog and cat playing,
You and I making love by the fire,
        That's my desire.


This is the paper that Kathy makes believe she's working on
when the boss leaves and she puts on her purple sunglasses,
makes the radio louder, and sits until she hears the bell on
the elevator, which means he's gone for the day and she can
watch out the window, call everyone and goof off, talk to her-
self and sing singsongs and go crazy until five and then get off!

46

## Life Is Beautiful

Life is beautiful
For people who don't look
At all the ugly things in life.

Some people think it's a fantasy
But to me trees, stars,
Water, rocks, rain—
Everything about nature is beautiful because it isn't false.


## Wishful Thinking

Freedom is the wish of many.
I wish I could be free
To enjoy the sun, flowers and trees.

The sun that never fails to rise
And to warm and light the way.
The brightness of the fall leaves—

Reds, yellows, oranges—
Blending into a beautiful rainbow.

The freedom of waking and walking down the road,
Hearing the birds sing,
Seeing nature as it should be.

I wish for a lot of things to be,
But most of all I wish
To be accepted
        For ME

## Nowhere

Is this what was
supposed to be
so wonderful?
Well, if it is, I
can tell you—
I feel nowhere.
You're on a different
channel and I
can't fix the TV to
focus you in
because you weren't
tuned in to the
right show.


## The Question

It feels strange without you.
Am I supposed to dig
the empty echo of the rooms?
Can't figure out where
it will end; I only hope
we don't get off
at different exits.

YESTERDAY
TODAY       **?**
TOMORROW **.**

## Stomach

No matter where I am or what I do,
all of a sudden a belly twister
sneaks in and I think of you.
Please stop! My stomach is upset
and I'm out of Alka-Seltzer.


## How Many Is Too Much?

How many is too much?
When will it stop?
The endless bomb of feelings
        that upset your role:

Who? When? How?
You? Him? Why?
Where is happiness?
Has it gotten lost in the shuffle?

I feel, I think, I put it aside.
Oh, people and places will take up my time,
But is it worth it?
That's blowing my mind.

I can be with you now,
but not really.
John doesn't like his merchandise,
but he won't return it to the store.
Money back guaranteed within seven days
but you lost out—
no one could find the receipt!

You want to own me like
a toy bought in the store,
to be played with until you desire it
no more, only to be cast aside for
a new pleasure.

But you can't do this to me—
For you see, I'm not John Bargain
Store material!


## Cars

Up and down like a yo-yo, my mind
is so tired,
so many cars on the road.
What are they to me?
I used to like cars, but I keep
getting run over and I'm starting to
get mad 'cause sometimes I feel
like I can't get up.
All you cars—fuck you.
Go take someone else for a ride.
I'd rather walk and maybe find
what I'm looking for,
Besides, this car is cracked up!

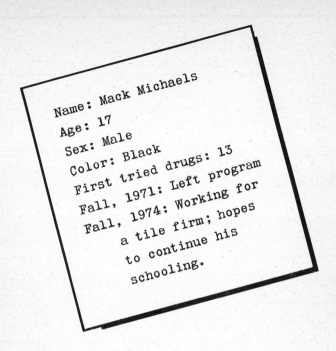

Name: Mack Michaels
Age: 17
Sex: Male
Color: Black
First tried drugs: 13
Fall, 1971: Left program
Fall, 1974: Working for
a tile firm; hopes
to continue his
schooling.

## Reflections

*I am a person who wants to be himself. It is hard for me to find out what is me. I can see other people not being themselves but can't accept that I am like that. When you have not found yourself, you start to believe that you are someone else. You believe your fantasies and that is what I did. Now I am starting to do and to feel, feeling feelings that I couldn't feel before. I am accepting the identity that is there. It is me.*

## To Hurt My Father

As I sat there and said I care,
I knew that I fooled you once again.
Not knowing what to say,
I lied.
Feeling bad, looking sad,
Not caring about anything,
Seeing how much you care.
Now you are hurt
And I am disappointed in myself.
Once again I feel I've
Never been able to finish anything.
I'm starting over.
I will become a man,
Live a life that I never lived before
By being myself.

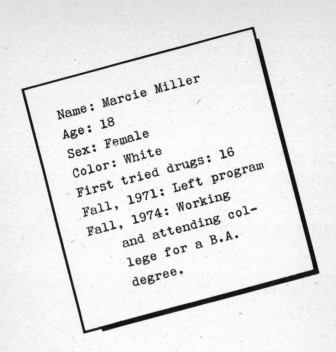

Name: Marcie Miller
Age: 18
Sex: Female
Color: White
First tried drugs: 16
Fall, 1971: Left program
Fall, 1974: Working
and attending col-
lege for a B.A.
degree.

## Reflections

*I'm eighteen. As of yet, my career is undecided. I'm either going to be a free-lance writer or a free-lance artist; most likely a writer. I'll decide while I'm going to college.*

*I've never been a very realistic person and it has caused me quite a bit of disillusionment, but I think I'll get more down-to-earth as I get older. For now it suits me fine. I know someday I will be married with children and a home of my own off in the wilderness somewhere far from any city. At this point I simply don't want it. There are too many other experiences in life I'd be missing out on.*

53

Only a fool will say he is aware
        of everything he does and why he does it
Because the mind is a strange machine
That won't let the animal of the heart
        Know all its secrets;
Otherwise the heart would break.
But you can learn to master your mind
Rather than be a slave to its absurd whims.
Living is for all who are—
But life is only for those that do.


## Antidote

You are snake, black venom, evil woman.
A dagger in the pit of me.
You try to smile pinkly but the pink turns red
and the red burns black.
You step over my shoulder into the page I am reading
or the poem I am writing and devour my courage,
So I stop writing, stop reading
and stare dumbly at the typewriter, ready to kill.
If you wanted trust, I could give it to you.
But you demand efficiency, accuracy, brevity . . . and such
        dedication.
No trust for you. Only credit forms, paper clips, and gossip
which you confidentially deliver with your loud claws.
You are a statistic.
Not even worth writing about
but your venom is instantaneously effective,
making the victim writhe in humiliation
as you deliver your smashing tour de force,
twisting his arm behind his back with your voice,
and smiling with your big teeth.
So this antidote is necessary
after only one bite, wishing my blood would leave my body.

## Tomorrow

Tomorrow is a beautiful woman with soft eyes
that say "I'm sorry" as you reach for her and she's gone.
But you really don't care because the eyes
made the difference,
And there's always tomorrow.


## The Rose Wilts

The rose wilts on a dying thorn of golden dead memories.
A dying thorn of gold—
You left it on my pillow
As I cried into the night.
Will it end, my self-created hell?
It sleeps silently within me,
Awakening like a little seemingly harmless bee in the wilted
    rose,
Flying straight to my heart
Stinging me with a poison—
A poison that makes the world look very ugly.
It's no longer raining purple and green jelly beans;
The rain is black and harsh and never ending.
A bed of roses and dynamite—
Life is a bed of roses and dynamite,
And I feel sometimes if one more thing happens to me,
If I learn another thing,
Grow a little more,
I will explode
Because I'm safe within a little shell of hell
Whenever I choose
And I think that little devil
The bee
Is going to kill me one day.

## Unfair

You are hiding and I want to find you,
but hide-and-seek with aluminum-foil swords just
isn't my game anymore—
Especially since you've got the swords
and I'm "It."


## In Memory

Her mother tried, all the neighbors said.
Her mother's dead now.
Still she goes on searching and the grave within her that her
    mother
started digging when she was born is now filled.
She brings flowers for her mother and her first love
every few months when she remembers.
They lie peacefully within her, side by side.


## Love Offering

In the valley a small flower grew.
I knew I shouldn't have picked it.
The sign did say, "This isn't yours. Don't take it."
But I imagined how your face would look when I gave it
    to you,
and since no one would miss it anyway, I took it.
It was a plastic flower, hard, pink and green, but I thought it
    wouldn't
matter to you since you would know what was in my mind
    when I picked it.
I ran to meet you.

When I tried to give it to you I realized you didn't know.
It was silly to forget that you don't know what I'm thinking
     all the time.
The pleased face I imagined was now like a dream I always
     forget upon
awakening; but I try to remember it anyway.
Instead you were embarrassed, pushing it away.
I still tried to give it to you.
I couldn't help thinking you would feel the same way I would
     if you'd
given me a flower. Your friends laughed and walked away.
Reconsidering, you took it, putting it in your pocket.

The next day, even though you showed me that you'd put
     it on your dresser,
it was too late.


## Search for Innocence

Where is the virgin Lily?
I seek her in far-off fields,
Lying in the grass staring at the sky,
Eyes open in flower-faced awe
Waiting for the rain.
Lily is dying and I haven't met her yet.
She's dying in the maze of a
Minotaur civilization that doesn't know
How to love her.
Mass-produced Madison Avenue Innocence
Is the offering of those
Who don't know the difference
Between natural love and money.

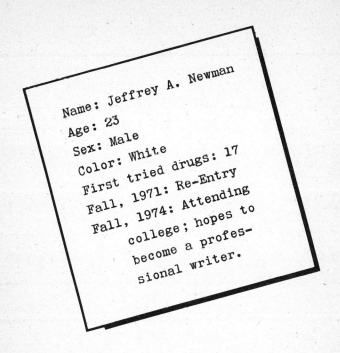

Name: Jeffrey A. Newman
Age: 23
Sex: Male
Color: White
First tried drugs: 17
Fall, 1971: Re-Entry
Fall, 1974: Attending
    college; hopes to
    become a profes-
    sional writer.

## Reflections

*Before I went into Samaritan Halfway Society, I had spent seven years of life using everything from grass to cocaine to heroin.*

*I have had two and a half years of college.*

*Originally I had this crazy thought that if I wrote an autobiography it would come out unhappy, but I'm not so sure now.*

## Apocalypse

The coming is now
Snow is the revolution in a child's eye.

## Thought Wheel

Planning is not real
Trying is losing
Being is beautiful
Thinking is a stream
Water is life
Life is death uncovered
Beauty is within.
Why is man the way he is?

## Western

Cowboy doesn't know anything
in my dream.

Life is simple—
just lyin' there
feelin' good,
night clouds passing

Filled with the sky
and wind from the desert,
he doesn't hope,
just is.

60

## Falling Apart

I feel the deepening need
to be held and loved
and become almost crazed
in anxiety.

My body trembles.
My voice quivers.

I want to be filled
or I don't want to live.

## Poem

Staying inside creates insanity, death.
Coming out is life and love.

## Poem

The feeling is lonely,
hating it and loving it.
Little boy, dope fiend
made friends with sadness,
scared and confused,

anxious and desperate for love,
knowing only a fix
and the security of madness,
with no end,
alone.

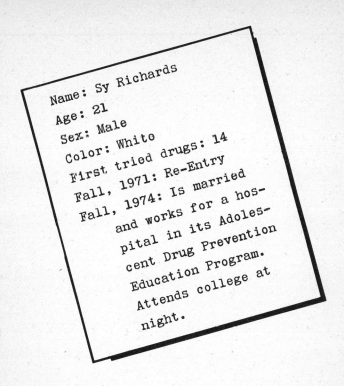

Name: Sy Richards
Age: 21
Sex: Male
Color: White
First tried drugs: 14
Fall, 1971: Re-Entry
Fall, 1974: Is married
and works for a hos-
pital in its Adoles-
cent Drug Prevention
Education Program.
Attends college at
night.

## Reflections

*Snowed in on a Friday night. And I thought winter was over and done with. Now I am faced with two choices: one, think about how things will be in a couple of weeks; two, think about the past. So, for now, I'll choose the latter.*

*I remember my first ten or twelve winters as sort of a big conglomeration of frozen fingers, slushy snowball fights, and rows of rubbers outside the classroom. Then there were the special Saturday-night sled rallies at "Dead Man's Hill," which, in the summer, returned*

to its primary function—the fairway of the seventh
hole (par 4) at the golf course. There were fantastic
eight- or nine-hour marathons of up-and-down com-
petition and you were a winner if you weren't the first
to say you were cold. The real hero, though, was the
guy who hit a bench and whose sled broke. Then
everyone would make it to the candy store for a hot
chocolate.

Then there were a couple of winters when I'd be
walking to the school-bus stop when it would hap-
pen, a snowflake! Bingo! I'd turn around, run home
and, without the least feeling of guilt, scream, "Ma,
no buses today! It's snowing." After the ensuing ar-
gument, I'd call "the gang" to see what they were
doing because I just knew the same scene was taking
place at their houses. We usually ended up taking
the bus to school and hanging out in the park across
the street.

I wish I could finish, but, you see, the snow has
stopped and I have to SHOVEL THE WALK!!!


## On the Street

On the street, well,
I was almost a human being,
At least on the outside I was.
Hunting, stalking, crying, wanting,
A life of "if only's" and "never's"
Only to end up with a needle in my arm
And on the nod.

How come I didn't know
the only way to be free
was just to be plain old me?

64

# To Be a Kid Again

To be a kid again and live it all over,
To not know the meaning of worry and responsibility
And to be content with just the sunshine and flowers
And frolic in the snow.
And escape the hustle and bustle
In the cover of our own little slush-built igloos.
To walk through the park barefoot, hunting rabbits
With flimsy hand-built bow and arrows.
To sit with the guys and build a campfire
That toasts your marshmallows and warms your soul,
To play skulby in the schoolyard
With your favorite crayon-filled bottlecap, and win!
To climb a tree
And perch yourself high on a limb
Above the grass and gaze at the people
Passing below you.
Content, satisfied, secure and happy.
And the anxious, excited feeling as you open your gifts on
    Christmas morning.
Or the taste of those Sunday afternoons.
Chocolate malteds after the ball game.
And who, disguised as Clark Kent, mild-mannered reporter
    for *The Daily Planet* . . .
Oh, wow! You remember the cartoons on Saturday mornings?
Or "The Little Rascals" just before you were sent off to school?

## The Fisherman

Long walk downhill on an early spring morn,
One more rise—there, the red sloop, the sail a little torn.
Life beginning to stir on either side of the road.
He raises his heavy head to the smell of a lawn freshly mowed.
He begins his work without even really thinking,
Not aware of himself or of the dead fish stinking.
He's out with the tide, the captain of his ship,
Examining hooks and nets, fixing every rip.
Bait's out, they're biting, the catch is good.
Working hard, sweat pouring to rotting wood.
Headed home now, he begins to unbend.
Tomorrow, at the same time, he will start once again.


## Thoughts

Sitting quietly by the sea,
A new day, same old me.
I wonder if things are going to change,
Sometimes life's easy, sometimes it's strange.
Wondering what's going on in me,
Trying to figure out what's going to be.
So many things to do, never enough time,
Everybody always racing for that extra dime.

Life is to live, of that I'm sure
And to be myself is what I'm living for.

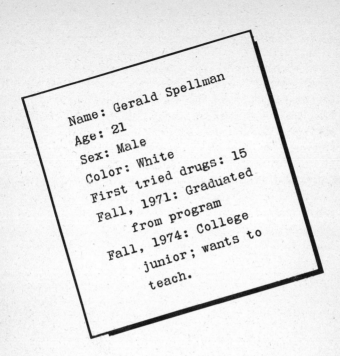

Name: Gerald Spellman
Age: 21
Sex: Male
Color: White
First tried drugs: 15
Fall, 1971: Graduated
     from program
Fall, 1974: College
     junior; wants to
teach.

## Reflections

*I started at the age of fifteen to use drugs and die.
At the age of nineteen I found hope with my first and
last arrest.*

## First Poem

She came dressed in sable
And sat down at the table,
Searching for a shade of the truth
And wearing around her neck the tooth
Of a tiger shark.

Tightly she clutched the pearly white
And wished and wished with all her might,
Searching for a shade of the truth
And wearing around her neck the root
Beneath the dark.


## Second Poem

To fear a place I do not know,
a shadow cast by a candle's glow,
the deadening silence from without,
the throbbing from within.
To hear the echoes of the past,
the wind brings back its ghost attacks.
Fury lashing at the soul,
the hollow hole beneath my chest is swelling
and my mind can't rest.
Mother Nature, please caress this emptiness,
surround me with your endless warmth, your timeless love,
and give me strength to be a man.

68

## Third Poem

When you have no place to turn,
And you're yearning to be free
And you're begging for concern,
And your burning eyes can't see,

I've found that you are you;
I've learned that I am me.

Misfortune is the difference,
Understanding is the key.


## Fourth Poem

It is society's game
To take you from childhood's airplane
Send you to school to wash your brain
Set up rules to make you insane
Take your happiness and remains
Stack them in a toy box locked with a chain
Then you're told not to complain.
You're sent out to the working plains
Where you go to fatigue your frame
Now you're savage, no longer tame
You put on your suit and look the same
Be grateful for being made a lame
Look how lucky you are to have a name
Always keep it in mind that money reigns
This crazy world should be ashamed
Could this be the reason for cocaine?

## Fifth Poem

To be lonely is to be lost
in the canyons of your mind
where the only thing you find is sorrow.
You drift aimlessly about
in the rivers of despair
where the only hope you find is tomorrow.

To be lonely is to be lost
in the ticking of a clock
where the only thing you hear
is rhythmic time.

To be lonely is to be lost
in the hollow candle glow
where the only hope you see
is fading rhyme.


## Everyone Who Passes

Crystal-clear lake and mountain streams
Look upon the fisherman's dream;
Floating garbage, oil slick, sand—
See what has happened
To our land.
Rust-eroded cans
On broken-bottled beach
Swim in polluted
saltwater bleach.
Greenwood-dying forest,
Playground of the masses
Garbage dump expanded
By everyone who passes.

70

## Mama

Your eyes shine like the morning mist on the mountainside
When the sun comes up to greet the day.
Your lips are like the evening kiss of the ocean tide
When the moon comes to meet the night.
Your tears fall like the autumn's wish that its leaves hide
When the earth numbs and greets the fading light.

Your life has been a bad one,
Your story is a sad one,
You've just begun to have some fun.
        The life you lead is better than none.


## God, but if This Ain't a Boss Window

God, but if this ain't a boss window.
Here I am just getting ready for bed,
It must be about two thirty.
It's raining now and I can hear a cricket
Making its lonely noise in the distance.
The rain is crawling like a snake
Falling to the earth
And absorbing whatever it touches.
This window,
Which I just finished painting, by the way, a pretty yellow,
Gives me a dynamite view of the grounds
Except for those fuckin' telephone wires.
There is a tree outside
And it really is beautiful—
Tall and crimson in color
With life from its new buds.
It's springtime and I'm in love.
I really only knew you for four short hours
And now a week later I can't forget you,

71

You're the first thing I think of in the morning
And the last thing at night.
It must be love.
I want to hold you tight and touch your pretty brown hair
And gaze into your warm green eyes
And kiss your lips soft as the petals of the flower
That I gave you when we parted.
I'm living on your memory
And everything else is hazy.
God, but if this ain't a boss window.


## Depression

Is there peace in silence, or only the rustling of leaves
in the backyard of the empty memories that you hold so dear
and cling to in your time of need?
Isn't silence the communion of your lonely thoughts and
    dreams
which you thrive on
and all of the frustration, aspirations, and anxieties that
    confine you
to the four walls which are the extent of your existence
and the chains of your deepest hopes?
Silence is the prison that breeds despair
where the light is dim and the debts are high
and the bail is not in sight.
It is the letter of acquittal that is always coming
in the mail tomorrow.
The sorrow and tears shed in righteous pity
for those waiting on death row
where the only sounds are echoing footsteps
and the jailer's keys.
The only peace there is in silence
comes when the rustling leaves are no longer
heard.

# Untitled

I am a lonely man tonight
As I walk the streets without you.
Trying to ignore the cold that I feel on my way home.
Thinking about what I told you the night before
And wondering, what for?
Did it make anything clear?
Was it what you wanted to hear?
To be hurt and sink into the fear
And drew apart when we were so near?
To find something too big for both of us to understand
And learning only a little bit more
to comprehend what we never can?
I am sorry that I hurt the only one who really cares,
The only spark of joy that my emptiness bears.
It hurts to keep my head up high
When I feel the weight of the tears you cry.
And I carry the shame of my selfish life
And I am scared to bring my pain into your life.

*(Poems Written in Re-Entry)*

# Introspection

A yellow daffodil lay dying in our bottle of Mateus
As I poked on my pipe and watched the smoke rise.
And I wondered what the sun would look like in the morning
Or if more rain would come.
Not really happy, and not really sad—
—kind of mellow and still—
wilting as did the yellow daffodil.

73

I think I'll take the curtains from my wall
and let my mind expand to the windowsill
where I'll make a window box and grow more daffodils
They will bring each new day in
With a subtle ring of their petal bells.
And when a cloudy night comes,
I'll have my own stars to wish by.


## Destiny's Alms

Isn't it tragic that Life sometimes seems empty
And the magic it takes to fill it is on the express train?
Is it that the cup is half full or half empty,
or rather that the cup *is*?
Can destiny and purpose exist together, or are they theories of
    two different realms that only cross in chaos?
I am now—
not tomorrow's dreams or yesterday's failures.
I am the cup at the banquet of meaning and
at the same time there for destiny's alms.
Life comes in rushes, with the shadow of death only a few
    steps behind.
So when you walk, don't look back—
For what is past is gone
And what is lost is time.


## Broken Wings

Oh, little girl, child, lover, born of dreams,
made of needs that make me scream
inside.
I'm never gonna let you hide.

Oh, little girl, grown, rover on the prowl,
afraid to bleed, you make me howl
outside.
Let your feelings be your guide.
Oh, little girl, lost over by and by,
too scared to see the reasons why we're here.
Don't ever be afraid of fear.
Oh, little girl, found out to cry and cry
too hurt and tired to want to fly
or care.
I'm fixing broken wings this year.


## Appointment with a Dream

How do you get ahead when the world around you is dying,
    or almost dead
When sights you've seen fill your head
and ads show the way to happiness
and you're always in the red?
When you find that you detest the life you lead
and there is no place left to rest?
Work your job, support your home,
keep up your car, take out a loan,
Work your fingers to the bone.
And as I sit and want to quit,
There is nothing more lonely than a clock.
And I realize that time is what I have the most of,
To think of better times to come
And time to be with you, my love.
My sorrow runs deep
Through city stone and lonely street
And I awake each day to keep
An appointment with a dream.

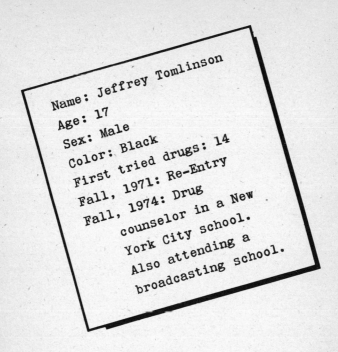

Name: Jeffrey Tomlinson
Age: 17
Sex: Male
Color: Black
First tried drugs: 14
Fall, 1971: Re-Entry
Fall, 1974: Drug
    counselor in a New
    York City school.
Also attending a
broadcasting school.

## Reflections

*Just recently I have been doing a lot of thinking about Samaritan, a lot of comparing between the "then" and the "now."*

*The people were so open then. I learned how to understand myself, my feelings. I learned how to look into what a person said in order to understand what he meant.*

*I find that there are not many people I can now honestly relate to or discuss my bona fide feelings*

77

*with and not be judged. It is not a matter of criticism [illegible] it is a matter of understanding.*

*So many people are playing so many games.*

*One of the things that bothers me is that so many people are hung up on material things. I understand the importance of being financially secure, and I know how the dollar can help you enjoy life. Yet, it is a matter of putting everything into its proper perspective, including money.*

*It is important to understand what part* you *play in directing your own happiness.*

## Mr. God

Hate, obsession, pain, anguish, fear, sorrow—
Damn!
I cannot see one intending it to be that way.
Mr. God, have the frustrated tears in my eyes, and the pain in my heart gone unnoticed for so many years?
If you can see, Mr. God, I say to you—
Set me Free!

## Poems of a Lost Love

I

There is nothing to be said,
No words to be shared
As we feel
The pain we created.

Like an endless road,
There seems to be no hope

That one day
We will open the gateway to happiness
As one—

## II

The sun shines,
Yet it is dark.
The forsythia
Sign of spring
Has arrived,
But my heart can't see it.
The children smile
And I cry—

# Freedom

Why—
Why do I want so bad to be thrust
Into this troubled world,
To have the freedom of a jungle?
Why does it mean so much to me
To stand alone,
Just to subject myself as prey
For the hungry
Death struggle,
The unjust savagery of man?
But as the sun rises to the darkness,
There is another side.
The majesty of a soft cloud on a spring day
Is beauty.
To love.

I am beginning to see now
How I may roam this savage jungle

Like a hunted animal;
Or I may soar through the skies
Like the green phoenix,
With the billowing wind as my companion.

I desire not
To be cast into this troubled world,
Only to roam like an animal.
Give me the sky
And the wind,
And let the roads be endless for me;
For in my lifetime
Let me not roam,
Adapt to the life of the jungle.
Allow me to look down and see that which I don't want,
And all I can have.